Spring Festivals

Helen Bliss

Photographs by Peter Millard

Contents

W

FRANKLIN WATTS

LONDON • SYDNEY

About Spring festivals

Spring is when we welcome new life after the winter. All of the activities in this book are inspired by the traditions of people around the world at springtime.

In Christian countries, there are several Spring festivals.

People celebrate Valentine's Day on 14th February by sending cards and small gifts to loved ones.

Mardi-Gras or carnival is celebrated with street parties where everyone dresses up and has fun.

On Mothering Sunday children give gifts of flowers and cards to their mother.

At Easter, Christians celebrate the resurrection of Jesus and decorate their churches with flowers, baby animals and eggs to represent new life.

At Whitsun, Christians celebrate the appearance of the Holy Spirit to the disciples of Jesus. The white dove is a symbol of the Holy Spirit.

May Day is an ancient pre-Christian festival to celebrate the beginning of spring. The Tree of Life represents new growth after winter.

Hindus celebrate the coming of spring at Holi. They have great fun throwing coloured water at each other and eating special food and sweets.

Purim is a Jewish festival when Queen Esther is remembered for saving the Jews from Haman, a wicked tyrant.

 Wherever you see this sign, it means that you should ask for help from an adult.

Valentine's Day cards

Get ready

✔ Coloured card   ✔ Scissors   ✔ Glue

✔ Envelope   ✔ Gummed paper   ✔ Pencil

...Get set

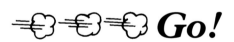

Cut a rectangle from the card.
Fold it in half so it fits into your envelope.
Cut out hearts and flowers
from the gummed paper.

⚞⚞⚞ *Go!*

Lick and stick the shapes
on to the front of the card.
Write a message inside.

Mardi-Gras masks

Get ready

- ✔ Tape measure
- ✔ Thin cardboard
- ✔ Scissors
- ✔ Small garden stick
- ✔ Crêpe paper
- ✔ Paint and brush
- ✔ Feathers
- ✔ Sequins

...Get set

Measure the width of your face.
Draw a mask shape like this
on the cardboard, to fit your face width.
Cut it out, including eye holes.

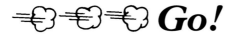 Go!

Tape the stick on to
one side of the mask.
Decorate the mask with
paints, sequins, feathers and crêpe paper.

Mothers' Day basket

Get ready

✔ Rectangle of coloured card (17cm x 18cm)

✔ Pencil and ruler
✔ Scissors and glue

...Get set

Draw a rectangle 5cm inside the cut card.
Cut along the dotted lines A, B, C and D
(see diagram).
Cut away the shaded area.
Cut a pretty edge to the rectangle.
Fold inwards on all the lines.
Cut a card handle 1cm x 24cm.

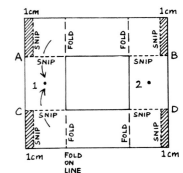

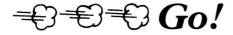 **Go!**

Glue the sides of the basket at points 1 and 2.
Glue the handle to the sides.
Decorate with card flowers and hearts.
Fill with treats.

Easter bonnet

Get ready

- ✔ Felt
- ✔ Pencil
- ✔ Needle and embroidery thread
- ✔ Sticky tape
- ✔ Scraps of felt
- ✔ Glue
- ✔ Scissors
- ✔ Sequins

...Get set

Measure round your head.
Cut a strip of felt this long
and 6cm wide.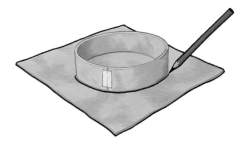
Tape the ends together to form a ring.
Place the felt ring on some felt.
Draw round the felt circle and cut it out.

 *Go!*

Carefully sew the long strip to the circle of felt.
Sew up the back of the hat.
Decorate with shapes cut from felt.

Easter biscuits

Get ready

- ✔ 230g flour
- ✔ 115g butter
- ✔ 115g sugar
- ✔ Beaten egg
- ✔ Squeeze of lemon
- ✔ Pinch of cinnamon
- ✔ Pinch of mixed spice
- ✔ Handful of currants
- ✔ Wooden board
- ✔ Rolling pin
- ✔ Pastry cutter
- ✔ Baking tray
- ✔ SET THE OVEN TO 190°C/375°F/GAS MARK 5

...Get set

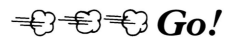

Rub the butter and flour together.
Add the rest of the ingredients, except the egg.
Then mix in the egg to form a dough.
Roll it out on a floured board to 1cm thickness.
Cut into biscuit shapes with a pastry cutter.

ᕦᕤᕦᕤᕦᕤ *Go!*

 Place on a greased baking tray.
Bake in the oven for 10–15 minutes.

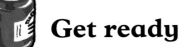

Easter egg rings

Get ready

✔ Cardboard tube   ✔ Paint and brush   ✔ Thin card

✔ Scissors   ✔ Pencil   ✔ Glue

...Get set

Cut a 3cm length from the cardboard tube.
Paint it a bright colour, inside and out.
Leave it to dry.

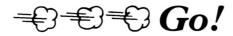

⇶ *Go!*

Draw animals and flowers on to card.
Paint them and cut them out when dry.
Glue the shapes on to the ring.

Whitsun dove

Get ready

✔ Thin card   ✔ White paper   ✔ Scissors

✔ Felt-tip pens   ✔ Cotton thread   ✔ Pencil

...Get set

Draw a dove shape on to the card.
Cut it out.
Cut a rectangle of paper.
Fold it back and forth like a fan.
Cut a slit in the body, like this:

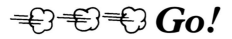 *Go!*

Push the paper fan through the slit.
This makes the wings.
Draw an eye on your dove with a felt-tip pen.
Hang it up with some thread.

Tree of Life

Get ready

✔ Card ✔ Cardboard tube ✔ Plasticine

✔ Masking tape ✔ Paint and brush ✔ Glue

✔ Scissors ✔ Coloured paper ✔ Pencil

...Get set

Cut slits into the side of a long cardboard tube.
Draw long branches on to card.
Tape them into each slit.
Paint the trunk and branches.
Put a lump of Plasticine into the bottom
of the trunk to weigh it down.

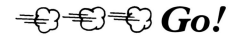 **Go!**

Cut the coloured paper into
flower, leaf and bird shapes.
Stick them on to the branches.

Barfi

Get ready

- ✔ 2 cups milk
- ✔ 1.5 cups sugar
- ✔ 2 cups milk powder
- ✔ 2 cups dessicated coconut
- ✔ 2 teaspsoons gelatine
- ✔ Few drops vanilla essence
- ✔ Large saucepan
- ✔ Wooden spoon
- ✔ Greased dish
- ✔ Chopped nuts to decorate

...Get set

Melt the gelatine in 4 tablespoons of hot water.
Simmer the milk, sugar and milk powder
in the saucepan, stirring all the time.
When the mixture thickens, take it from the heat.
Add the coconut, gelatine and vanilla essence.
Stir it well.

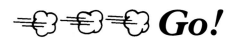 **Go!**

Pour the mixture into the greased dish.
Chill until set, then sprinkle with chopped nuts.

Queen Esther's crown

Get ready

✔ Card
✔ Paint and brush
✔ Shiny paper

✔ Tape measure
✔ Pencil
✔ Foil sweet wrappers

✔ Scissors
✔ Sticky tape

...Get set

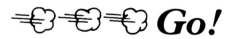

Measure round your head
Add 3cm to this measurement.
Draw a rectangle this long and 15cm high,
with a crown pattern along the top of it.
Cut it out and tape at the back to fit your head.

❄ ❄ ❄ *Go!*

Glue on foil and shiny paper
to decorate your crown.

Index

This edition 2003
Franklin Watts
96 Leonard Street
London EC2A 4XD

Franklin Watts Australia
45-51 Huntley Street
Alexandria
NSW 2015

©1993 Watts Books

Editor: Pippa Pollard

Design: Ruth Levy
Cover design: Mike Davis
Artwork: Ruth Levy

ISBN 0 7496 5240 3

A CIP catalogue record for this
book is available from the
British Library

Printed in Malaysia

Acknowledgements:
The author and publisher
would like to thank Camilla,
Julia, Madeleine, Mimi and
Raphael for their participation
in the photography of this
book.

24